This book is dedicated to all the great Therapy Dogs who improve the lives of humans and the Handlers who help them to be their best. You truly make the world a better place.

Pages, Pens & Paws

Moxy Makes a Difference © 2022 Nicole Selby

All rights reserved. No parts of this publication may be reproduced or transmitted in any form or by any means, electronically or mechanically including photocopying, recording, or any information or retrieval system, without prior written permission of the author.

ISBN: 978-1-989506-60-8

Design: Kira Alexanian

Cover Design: Kira Alexanian

Published in Canada

www.pagespenspaws.com

@author.nicoleselby

MOXY makes a DIFFERENCE

Writtten by **Nicole Selby** & **Tonya Cartmell**

Illustrated by **Kira Alexanian**

"Great job, Moxy! You made everyone so happy today," mom said with a smile as she removed my red Therapy Dog vest.

I touched her cheek with my nose which made her giggle before I went and laid down on my bed.

Hi! My name is Moxy, and I am a Therapy Dog. It is an important job; I visit nursing homes, hospitals, schools, and libraries four times a week with my mom. I meet so many different people (that are young and old!).

I do my best to make them smile and even help some of them work through hard situations and feelings.

My days are filled with pets, snuggles, treats, car rides, and listening to people's stories. Every day is different and usually lots of fun. Sometimes I need a nap as being a Therapy Dog is hard work.

Elementary schools are one of my favourite places to visit! One school that I visited had a brown, blue, and yellow tent with a thick, soft, red mat inside for me to lie on; the red mat matches my vest.

Sometimes when I arrive, the whole class comes running to see me! All my mom can see is my tail wiggling underneath all the hands petting me.

Once I'm inside the special tent, the children take turns coming to sit with me and they bring books for us to read together...well, they read and I listen, it's the best part of my day!

There is a boy who is very special to me, even though it has been a few years since I have seen him. His name is Jordyn, and I would love to tell you his story.

I met Jordyn on the first day of class at his new school; when my mom and I walked into the classroom, Jordyn ran to the back of the room. I could see how surprised he was to see a dog, and I could tell that he was afraid of me.

I looked at my mom to see if I had done anything to frighten him.

My mom said, "It's okay, Moxy. Jordan is afraid of dogs; he wasn't expecting to see one at school today. Let's give him some space and time. I'm sure he'll grow to love you like the other children."

Jordyn's teacher invited him to sit on the carpet in the circle with the other children, but Jordyn wasn't ready yet.

She told the children who I was and that I was there so they could take turns reading to me in the special tent.

While the other children came into the tent one at a time and read to me, Jordyn watched from the back of the classroom.

I loved listening to their stories. Some children were great readers and some stumbled over the words, but they did their best and they all got a snuggle from me when they were done.

The next week when we went back, I noticed that Jordyn moved a little closer so that he could see all the children coming into the tent to read to me.

I stayed quiet and still while they read.

After a few weeks, Jordyn asked if he could read a story to me. He sat far away, his hands trembled, and his voice shook, but he did it.

I was so proud of him. I gave him my best smile when he was done.

Jordyn was getting braver. The next time he read to me, he sat closer, and his voice was louder and steady. His hands shook a little bit, but when he was done, he smiled at me.

For the first time, Jordyn gave me a smile. I was so happy that my little tail wagged so hard my whole body wiggled.

The most exciting moment was the day Jordyn walked slowly into the reading tent and sat down across from me. I was worried that I might scare him; I stayed so still that I looked like a statue.

His voice was quieter, and his hands shook a little bit again, but he finished the whole story.

His teacher smiled and my mom had happy tears in her eyes.

The next week, Jordyn was waiting for me when I arrived in his classroom. While I said hello to all the children on the carpet, he showed my mom the book he had brought to read to me.

He even put his arm around me and whispered in my ear that I was his new friend.

I was so proud to see him overcome his fear.

I gave my new friend a nuzzle and blinked my big brown eyes at him.

One summer day, after I was done working with Jordyn's class, my mom and I were walking in the park when I heard a boy laughing. I knew the laugh belonged to Jordyn and looked around for him.

In the distance I saw a boy running with a brown curly haired dog.

They were playing together, jumping, and falling onto the grass.

My Jordyn now had a dog of his own.

My mom leaned down, gave me a hug, and said,

"That is because of you, Moxy, my beautiful girl."

This is one of the things I am most proud of in my work as a Therapy Dog.

Discussion Questions:

1. Moxy is a Doberman Pinscher who worked as a Therapy Dog. Can you think of some other jobs that the Doberman Pinscher breed is known for?

2. Doberman Pinschers have two main colors that they can be born with, black or red. Do you know which one Moxy was? Have you ever met a Doberman in real life?

3. Why do you think it was important for Moxy to show that her breed can be a great Therapy Dog? What is a prejudice?

4. In the story, Jordyn is afraid of dogs. How would a fear of dogs make it hard for a person to live their life?

5. In the story, Moxy gave Jordyn time to make his own decision on whether to read to her or not. Why is it important to let people face their fears and build confidence at their own pace? How can we help them to do that?

6. How do you think Moxy changed Jordyn's life? What might have happened if Jordyn never met Moxy?

Therapy Dog Moxy came to Nicole as a puppy in 2010, and she was certified as a Therapy Dog in 2012. Moxy quickly won over the heart of their community as this big, ferocious looking Doberman Pinscher showed the world that no matter your looks, it's what's on the inside that counts. Moxy was a regular participant in all the Therapy Dog program offered, giving her love and attention to young and old. Moxy could "read the room" better than most, teaching Nicole to trust Moxy's instincts and let her take the lead on who needed her most. When she passed away at the early age of 6 from a congenital condition the whole community mourned. Memorials were made, donations sent in her name, and dogs named in her honour. As a Therapy Dog she was among the greats, and she will never be forgotten.

Author Nicole Selby has always had a great love and respect for the ways animals support humans. Children's literacy has always been a passion of hers, especially when combined with reading to a Therapy Dog. As a child, Nicole could be found lost in a book and she hopes to foster that same love of reading in children across the world.

Author Tonya Cartmell was honoured to be involved in this project with Nicole to help promote the work the Therapy Dogs do. She lives in Caledonia with her husband, their rescued dog and two adopted cats. Tonya believes animal therapy can have a positive impact on people.

Illustrator Kira Alexanian has always found enjoyment in children's books from a young age – comforted by the heartwarming stories and playful, whimsical imagery. Her nanny Elaine, an artist, creative, and child-at-heart, is one of Kira's biggest inspirations.

Kira is currently studying Studio Art at the University of Guelph and is endlessly appreciative for the opportunity to support the great work of Therapy Dogs, while taking an exciting new step in her artistic career.

kira.alexanian@gmail.com

@kirasartwork

Manufactured by Amazon.ca
Bolton, ON

39070438R00021